Piano • Vocal • Guitar

American Folksongs & Spirituals

75 Songs of the American Heritage

ISBN 0-7935-5921-9

4/97 18538815

HAL•LEONARD® CORPORATION
7777 W. BLUEMOUND RD. P.O. BOX 13819 MILWAUKEE, WI 53213

O9-CFS-598

American Folksongs & Spirituals

Contents

Folksongs

Spirituals

ALL THE PRETTY LITTLE HORSES

Southeastern American Folksong

Gently

Hush - you - bye, don't you cry, go to sleep-y, lit - tle ba - by. When you wake, you shall have all the pret-ty lit-tle hors - es. Blacks and bays, dap-ples and greys, coach and six-a-lit-tle hors - es. Hush-you-bye, don't you cry, go to sleep-y, lit-tle ba - by.

ARKANSAS TRAVELER

Southern American Folksong

ANIMAL FAIR

American Folksong

AURA LEE

Words by W.W. FOSDICK
Music by GEORGE R. POULTON
First published in 1861

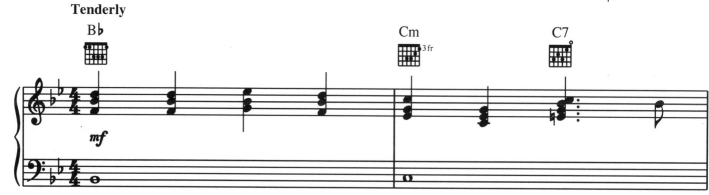

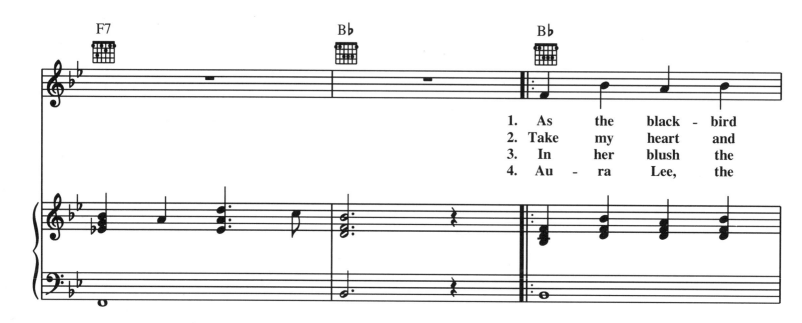

1. As the black - bird
2. Take my heart and
3. In her blush and the
4. Au - ra Lee, the

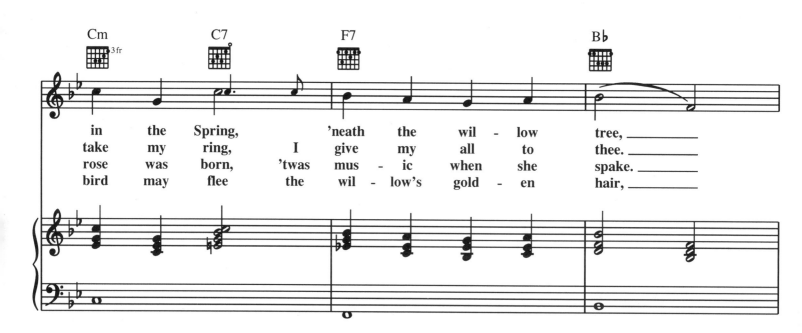

in the Spring, 'neath the wil - low tree,_____
take my ring, I give my all to thee._____
rose was born, 'twas mus - ic when she spake._____
bird may flee the wil - low's gold - en hair,_____

BLACK IS THE COLOR OF MY TRUE LOVE'S HAIR

Southern Appalachian Folksong

BLOW THE CANDLES OUT

American Folksong

THE BLUE TAIL FLY
(JIMMY CRACK CORN)

Folk version of a
minstrel song by DAN EMMETT
*(Emmett's song was
first published in 1846.)*

THE BOLL WEEVIL

Texas Folksong, c. 1890

Moderately fast

1. Oh, the boll wee-vil is a lit-tle black bug, comes from Mex-i-co, they say. Came all the way to Tex-as, came a-look-in' for a place to
(2.) first time I saw that lit-tle black bug, he was sit-tin' on a plant. I said, hey there, boll wee-vil, if you think you're gon-na stay, you
(3.) next thing I knew, that lit-tle black bug crawled a-round with-out a care, he was might-y well con-tent-ed, 'cause he had his fam-'ly
(4.) mad and I told the lit-tle black bug, gon-na spray you till y'all die, and the wee-vil said, if you do it, my pals will come and mul-ti-
(5.) got on my knees, Boll Wee-vil, said I, you're a-treat-in' me with scorn. You done et up my cot-ton, and you're start-in' on my field of
(6.) mer-chants came 'round to buy the cot-ton crop, I did-n't have a bale to sell. I could-n't pay the mort-gage, and heav-i-ly in debt I

BUFFALO GALS
(WON'T YOU COME OUT TONIGHT?)

Words and Music by
COOL WHITE (JOHN HODGES)
First published 1844

danced with a gal with a hole in her stock - ing and her

heel kept a - rock - in' and her toe kept a - knock - in. I

danced with a gal with a hole in her stock - ing, and we

danced by the light of the moon. moon.

BURY ME NOT
ON THE LONE PRAIRIE

Cowboy Ballad, c. 1870s
Attributed to H. CLEMENS of South Dakota
A parody based on the 1849 song "The Ocean Burial"
Words by Rev. EDWIN H. CHAPIN
Music by OSSIAN N. DODGE

CINDY

Southern Appalachian Folksong

CLEMENTINE

Mining Song, probably from California
Attributed to PERCY MONTROSE
1863 or 1883 (the date is obscured)

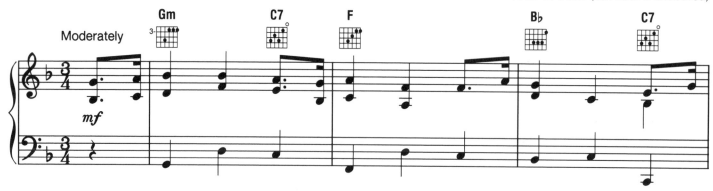

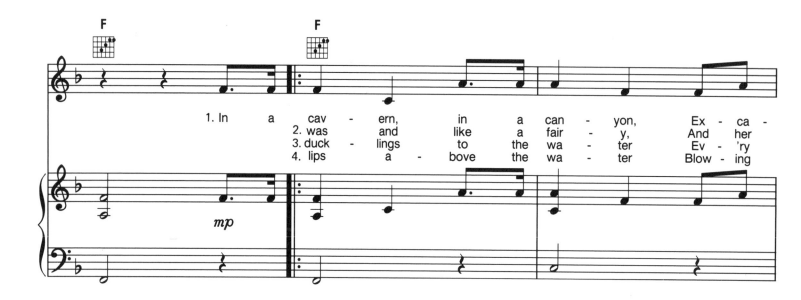

1. In a cav - ern, in a can - yon, Ex - ca -
2. was and like a fair - y, And her
3. duck - lings to the wa - ter Ev - 'ry
4. lips a - bove the wa - ter Blow - ing

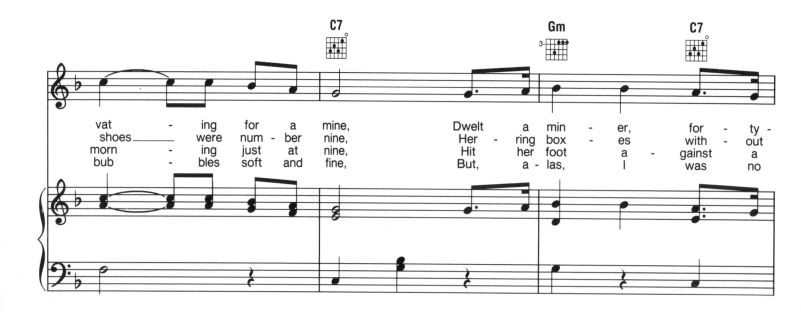

vat - ing for a mine, Dwelt a min - er, for - ty-
shoes were num - ber nine, Her - ring box - es with - out
morn - ing just at nine, Hit her foot a - gainst a
bub - bles soft and fine, But, a - las, I was no

COME ALL YE FAIR AND TENDER MAIDENS

Kentucky Folksong

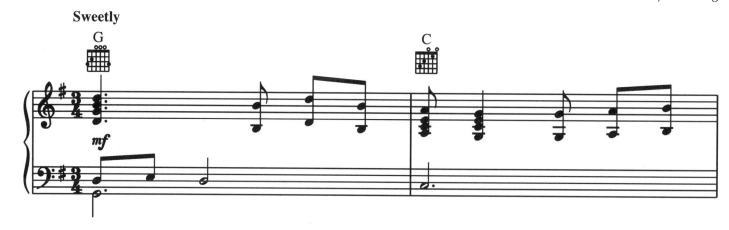

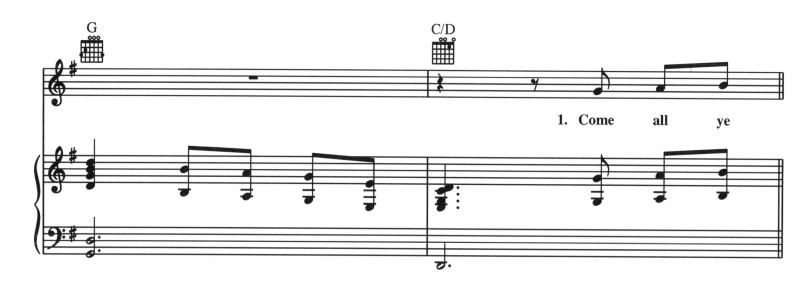

1. Come all ye

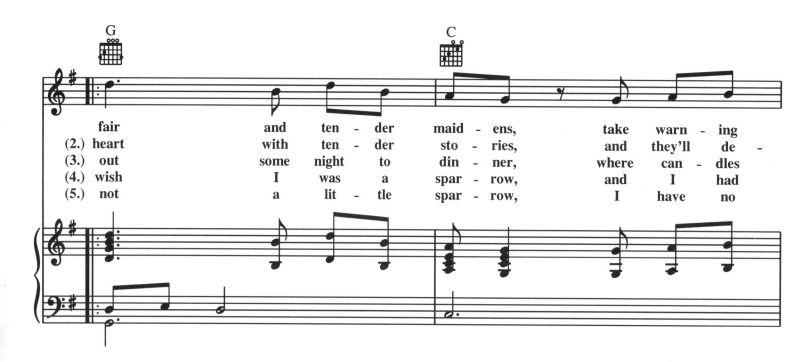

fair   and ten - der maid - ens,   take warn - ing
(2.) heart   with ten - der sto - ries,   and they'll de -
(3.) out   some night to din - ner,   where can - dles
(4.) wish   I was a spar - row,   and I had
(5.) not   a lit - tle spar - row,   I have no

Additional Lyrics

6. Come all ye fair and tender maidens,
Take warning how you court young men.
One night they may shine like stars above you,
To love you that night— but ne'er again.

7. If I had known before he courted,
That love was such a killing thing,
I'd a-locked my heart in a chest of iron,
And tied it down so it couldn't take wing.

COTTON-EYE JOE

Tennessee Folksong

Wistfully

1. Where did you come from, where did you go?
2. Come for to see you, come for to sing,

Where did you come from, ___ Cot-ton - Eyed ___ Joe?
Come for to show you my

dia - mond ___ ring.

DOWN IN THE VALLEY

Written by an anonymous
19th century prisoner of
the Raleigh State Prison as a letter
to a girl in Birmingham; the ballad
was published in newspapers across
the country

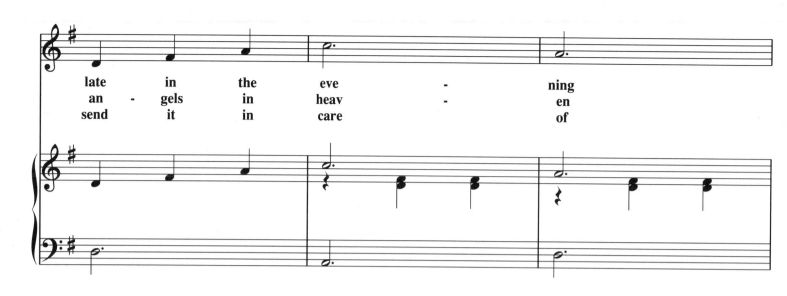

late in the eve - ning
an - gels in heav - en
send it in care of

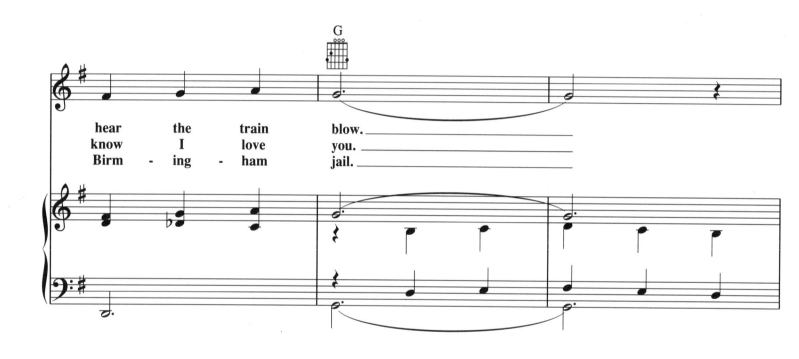

hear the train blow._____
know I love you._____
Birm - ing - ham jail._____

Hear that train blow - ing,
Know I love you,   dear,
Birm - ing - ham jail - house,

THE CRUEL WAR IS RAGING

American Folksong
from the Civil War

Moderately slow

1. The

cruel war is rag - ing, John - ny has to fight. I
(2.) go to your cap - tain, get down on my knees, and
(3.) mor - row is Sun - day, Mon - day is the day, that your
(4.) tie back my hair, men's cloth - ing I'll put on, and I'll
(5.) John - ny, oh, John - ny, I fear you are un - kind, for I

want to be with him from morn - ing till night. I
ten thou - sand gold gui - neas I'd give for your re - lease. Ten
cap - tain will call you, and you must o - bey. Your
pass as your com - rade as we march a - long. I'll
love you far bet - ter than all of man - kind. I

THE DRUNKEN SAILOR

American Sea Chantey

Additional Lyrics

Take him an' shake 'im, an' try an' wake i'm,
Earlye in the mornin'!

Give him a taste o' the bosun's rope-end,
Earlye in the mornin'!

Give him a dose o' salt an' water,
Earlye in the mornin'!

THE ERIE CANAL

Anonymous New York Work Song, c. 1820
(The Erie Canal, from Albany to Buffalo, opened in 1825.)

FRANKIE AND JOHNNY

Anonymous Blues Ballad
possibly from St. Louis or Kansas City
(There were many versions of the song,
with different lovers' names; this is
the version that became popular.)

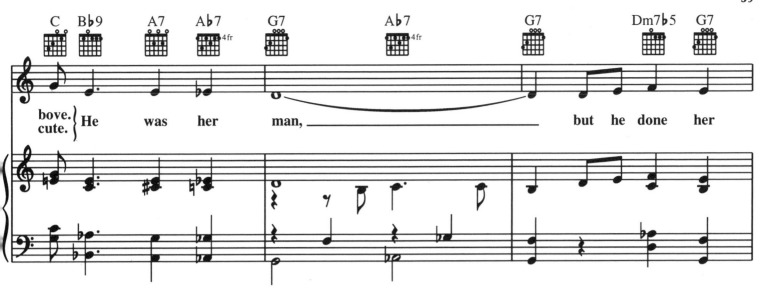

He was her man, _____ but he done her

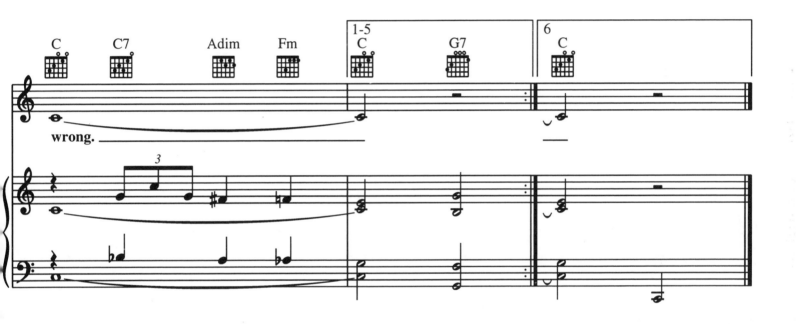

wrong. _____

Additional Lyrics

3. Johnny said, "I've got to leave now,
   But I won't be very long
   Don't sit up and wait for me, honey,
   Don't you worry while I'm gone;"
   He was her man, but he done her wrong.

4. Frankie went down to the hotel,
   Looked in the window so high,
   There she saw her lovin' Johnny
   Making love to Nellie Bly,
   He was her man, but he done her wrong.

5. Johnny saw Frankie a-comin',
   Down the back stairs he did scoot,
   Frankie, she took out her pistol,
   Oh that lady sure could shoot!
   He was her man, but he done her wrong.

6. Frankie, she went to the big chair,
   Calm as a lady could be,
   Turning her eyes up, she whisper'd,
   "Lord, I'm coming up to Thee,
   He was my man, but he done me wrong."

GIT ALONG, LITTLE DOGIES

Western American Cowboy Song

1. As I was a-walk-ing one
2. Ear-ly in spring we round
3. Whoop-ing and yell-ing and

morn-ing for pleas-ure I saw a cow-punch-er come
up all the dog-ies. We mark 'em and brand 'em and
round-ing the dog-ies from sun-rise till sun-set and

HOME ON THE RANGE

Kansas Folksong, c. 1873
possibly written by
DR. BREWSTER HIGLEY (words)
and DAN KELLY (music)

Additional Lyrics

3. Where the air is so pure and the zephyrs so free,
   And the breezes so balmy and light;
   Oh, I would not exchange my home on the range
   For the glittering cities so bright.
   To Chorus

4. Oh, give me a land where the bright diamond sand
   Flows leisurely down with the stream,
   Where the graceful white swan glides slowly along,
   Like a maid in a heavenly dream.
   To Chorus

HIGH BARBAREE

American Sea Chantey
sometimes attributed to CHARLES DIBDIN

Rollicking

1. There were two loft - y ships from old Eng - land ____
(2.) loft ____ there, a - loft! our ____ jol - ly boat - swain
(3.) naught up - on the stern, there's ____ naught up - on the
(4.) hail ____ her! O hail her! our gal - lant cap - tain
(5.) I am not a man - o'- war or a priv - a - teer," said

6., 7. *(See additional lyrics)*

came,
cries,
lee,"
cried,"
he,

Blow high! Blow low! An' so ____ sailed ____

Additional Lyrics

6. O, 'twas broadside to broadside a long time we lay,
   Blow high! Blow low! An' so sailed we.
   Until the Prince of Luther shot the pirate's masts away.
   All a-cruisin' down the coasts of the High Barbaree!

7. "O quarter! O quarter! those pirates then did cry,
   Blow high! Blow low! An' so sailed we.
   But the quarter that we gave them - we sunk them in the sea.
   All a cruisin' down the coasts of the High Barbaree!

HUSH, LITTLE BABY

Folk Lullaby from the Carolinas

THE HOUSE OF THE RISING SUN

Southern American Folksong

HOW CAN I KEEP FROM SINGING

American Folk Hymn

I'VE BEEN WORKING ON THE RAILROAD

American Folksong of obsure origins
(It possibly began as a minstrel song,
1860-1880, with additions and adaptations.)

With Vigor

I've been work-ing on the rail - road, all the live - long day; I've been work-ing on the rail - road, just to pass the time a - way.

JESSE JAMES

Anonymous Song from Missouri
about the notorious outlaw, killed in 1882

1. Jes-se James was a lad who __ killed man-y a man. Once he robbed the Glen-dale __ train. He would steal from the rich, he would give to the poor, had a hand and a heart and a

(2.) James was a friend, and he helped ev-'ry-one out with the loot he stole from the bank. When a rob-b'ry oc-cured, no one had __ a doubt, it was he and his dear broth-er

(3.) James took a name, "Jim-my How-ard", and flew to a town where he was-n't known. But his friend Rob-ert Ford, neith-er faith-ful nor true, turned a-gainst him and caught him a-

JOHN HENRY

Anonymous Song from West Virginia, 1870s
(John Henry was a railroad steel driver.
The legend tells of a contest between Henry,
working with a hammer, and a machine
team drill. Henry lost.)

Moderate folk-blues

Well,____ ev' - ry Mon - day____

2-8. (See additional lyrics)

morn - ing   when the blue - birds be -

gin to sing,   You can

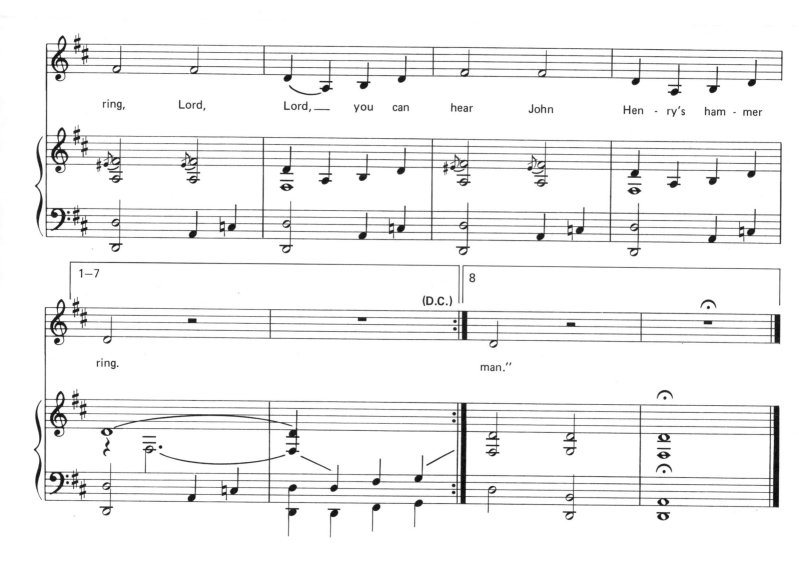

ring, Lord, Lord, ___ you can hear John Hen - ry's ham - mer

1—7 ring. (D.C.) **8** man."

Additional Lyrics

When John Henry was a little baby,
A-sitting on his papa's knee,
He picked up a hammer and a little
     piece of steel,
Said, "Hammer's gonna be the death
     of me"...

Well, the captain said to John Henry,
"Gonna bring me a steam drill 'round,
Gonna bring me a steam drill out on
     the job,
Gonna whup that steel on down"...

John Henry said to his captain,
"A man ain't nothin' but a man,
And before I let that steam drill beat
     me down,
I'll die with a hammer in my hand"...

John Henry said to his shaker,
"Shaker, why don't you pray?
'Cause if I miss this little piece of
     steel,
Tomorrow be your buryin' day...

John Henry was driving on the mountain
And his hammer was flashing fire.
And the last words I heard that poor boy
     say,
"Gimme a cool drink of water 'fore I die"...

John Henry, he drove fifteen feet,
The steam drill only made nine.
But he hammered so hard that he broke
     his poor heart,
And he laid down his hammer and he died...

They took John Henry to the graveyard
And they buried him in the sand.
And every locomotive comes a-roaring
     by says,
"There lies a steel-driving man"...

OLD JOE CLARK

Tennessee Folksong

1. Old Joe Clark, the preach-er's son, preached all o-ver the plain; The
3,5. *(See additional lyrics)*

on-ly text he ev-er used was high low jack and the game.

Chorus

Round and a-round, Old Joe Clark, round and a-round, I say; He'd

Additional Lyrics

3. When I was a little girl,
   I used to play with toys;
   Now I am a bigger girl,
   I'd rather play with boys. (Chorus)

4. When I was a little boy,
   I used to want a knife;
   Now I am a bigger boy,
   I only want a wife. (Chorus)

5. Wish I was a sugar tree,
   Standin' in the middle of some town;
   Ev'ry time a pretty girl passed,
   I'd shake some sugar down. (Chorus)

6. Old Joe had a yellow cat,
   She would not sing or pray;
   She stuck her head in a buttermilk jar
   And washed her sins away. (Chorus)

7. I wish I had a sweetheart;
   I'd set her on the shelf,
   And ev'ry time she'd smile at me
   I'd get up there myself. (Chorus)

LI'L LIZA JANE

American Folk Ballad
possibly from Maryland

1. I know a gal that I a - dore,
2. Down where she lives that the po - sies grow,
3. *See additional lyrics*

Li'l Li - za Jane. 'Way down south in
Li'l Li - za Jane. Chick - ens 'round the

Bal - ti - more, Li'l Li - za Jane.)
kitch - en door, Li'l Li - za Jane.)

Additional Lyrics

3. I wouldn't care how far we roam, Li'l Liza Jane,
   Where she's at is home sweet home, Li'l Liza Jane.
   Oh, Eliza, Li'l Liza Jane!
   Oh, Eliza, Li'l Liza Jane

OH! SUSANNA

Words and Music by
STEPHEN COLLINS FOSTER
First published 1848

THE OLD CHISHOLM TRAIL

Texas Cowboy Song
*(The Chisolm Trail was a cattle drive
route from San Antonio to Dodge City, Kansas,
where the herds were sold to market.)*

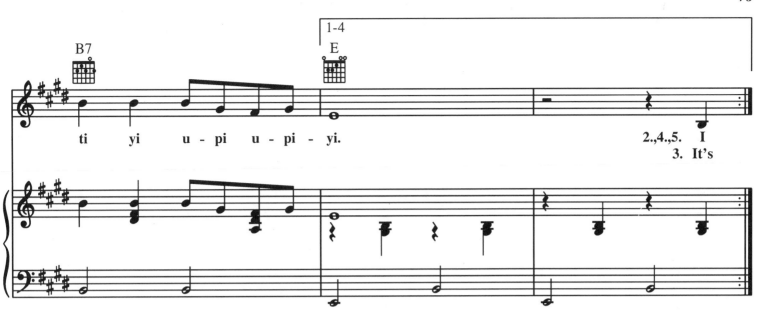

ti yi u - pi u - pi - yi.

2.,4.,5. I
3. It's

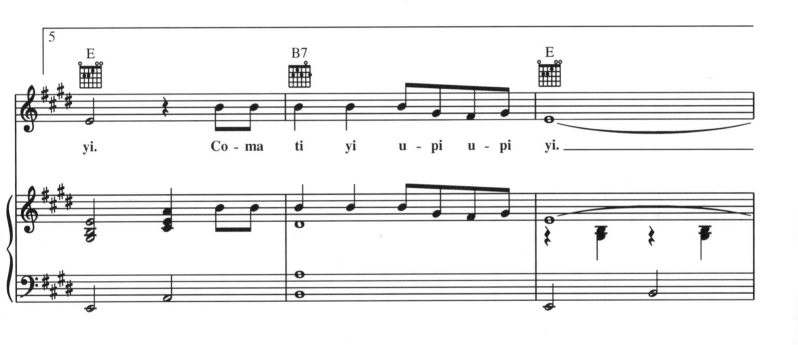

yi. Co - ma ti yi u - pi u - pi yi. _____

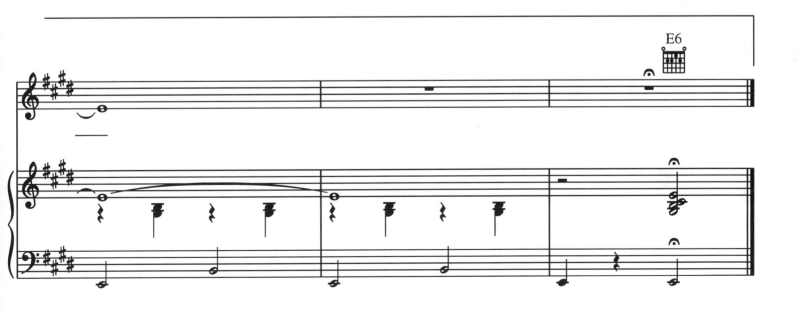

ON TOP OF OLD SMOKY

Kentucky Mountain Folksong

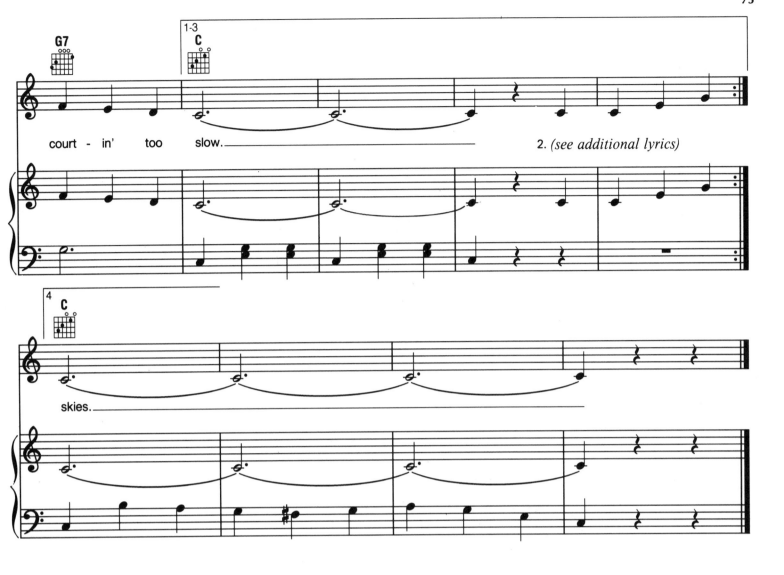

court - in' too slow._____ 2. *(see additional lyrics)*

skies._____

2. A-courtin's a pleasure,
A-flirtin's a grief,
A false-hearted lover -
Is worse than a thief.

3. For a thief, he will rob you,
And take what you have,
But a false-hearted lover -
Sends you to your grave.

4. She'll hug you and kiss you,
And tell you more lies,
Than the ties on the railroad,
Or the stars in the skies.

ONCE I HAD A SWEETHEART

Southern Appalachian Folksong

POLLY WOLLY DOODLE

Traditional American Minstrel Song

Bright, with humor

1. Oh, I

F

went down South for to see my Sal, Sing-ing pol-ly-wol-ly-doo-dle all the
2. Sal she is a__ maid-en fair, Sing-ing pol-ly-wol-ly-doo-dle all the
3. grass-hop-per sit-tin' on a rail-road track, Sing-ing pol-ly-wol-ly-doo-dle all the

C7

day. My__ Sal she is a spunk-y gal, Sing-ing
day. With__ curl-y eyes and laugh-ing hair, Sing-ing
day. A-pick-in' his teeth with a car-pet tack, Sing-ing

4. Oh, I went to bed, but it wasn't no use,
   Singing polly-wolly-doodle all the day.
   My feet stuck out like a chicken roost,
   Singing polly-wolly-doodle all the day.
   Chorus

5. Behind the barn down on my knees,
   Singing polly-wolly-doodle all the day.
   I thought I heard a chicken sneeze,
   Singing polly-wolly-doodle all the day.
   Chorus

6. He sneezed so hard with the whooping cough,
   Singing polly-wolly-doodle all the day.
   He sneezed his head and tail right off,
   Singing polly-wolly-doodle all the day.
   Chorus

THE RED RIVER VALLEY

Traditional American Cowboy Song
(Believed to be about the valley between Oklahoma
and Texas, or alternatively, about the Red River
of the North that flows from Minnesota and
the Dakotas to Lake Winnipeg.)

SHENANDOAH

American Folksong
about the Shenandoah Valley of Virginia
(Various versions exist, some about an
Iroquois chief and his daughter; a later, 19th
century sea chantey version was sometimes
sung for weighing anchor.)

SEEING NELLIE HOME

Words by J. FLETCHER
Music by FRANCES KYLE
1860s

SHE'LL BE COMIN' 'ROUND THE MOUNTAIN

originally a pre-Civil War
African-American Spiritual
"When the Chariot Comes,"
anonymously adapted by either
mountaineers or rail workers c. 1880s-1890s
("She" refers to a train locomotive.)

Brightly, with spirit

1. She'll be com - in' 'round the moun - tain when she
   driv - in' six white hors - es when she

comes; _____ she'll be com - in' 'round the
comes; _____ she'll be driv - in' six white

moun - tain when she comes. _____ She'll be
hors - es when she comes. _____ She'll be

Additional Lyrics

3. She'll be wearing red pajamas when she comes...
4. We will all go down to meet her when she comes...
5. We'll be singin' hallelujah when she comes...

SHOO FLY, DON'T BOTHER ME

Nonsense Game Song of
the Civil War period

SHORT'NIN' BREAD

Plantation Song from the American South

Rhythmically

Verse lyrics:

1. Put on the skil-let, put on the lead, mam-my's gon-na bake a lit-tle short-nin' bread. _ That ain't all ___ she's gon-na do, ___ Mam-my's gon-na make a pot of
2. Two lit-tle chil-lun ly-in' in bed, one of them was ail-in' and the oth-er 'most dead! Sent for the doc-tor, doc-tor said, _ got to feed them chil-lun some _
3. Snuck in the kitch-en, lift-ed the lead, filled my pock-ets up with short-'nin' bread. _ On the day ___ that I get wed, _ hope to have a gal who's good at

SIMPLE GIFTS

Traditional Shaker Song

Plaintively

'Tis a gift to be sim-ple, 'tis a

gift to be free, 'tis a gift to come down

where you ought to be, and when we find our-selves in the

SKIP TO MY LOU

19th Century American Game Song

Lou, Lou, Skip to my Lou, Lou, Lou, Skip to my Lou,

Lou, Lou, Skip to my Lou, Skip to my Lou, my dar - ling.

1. Lost my part - ner, what'll I do? Lost my part - ner, what'll I do?
2, 3, 4, 5, 6

2. I'll find another one, prettier than you,
   I'll find another one, prettier than you,
   I'll find another one, prettier than you,
   Skip to my Lou, my darling.

3. Little red wagon, painted blue.

4. Can't get a red bird, a blue bird'll do.

5. Cows in the meadow, moo, moo, moo.

6. Flies in the buttermilk, shoo, shoo, shoo.

SOURWOOD MOUNTAIN

Southern Appalachian Folksong

THE STREETS OF LAREDO

American Cowboy Song
based on the Irish ballad
"A Handful of Laurel"

With a lilt

1. As I _____ walked out in the
(2.) see by your out - fit that
(3.) once in the sad - dle I
(4.) six of my bud - dies to
(5.) beat the drum slow - ly and
6.,7. *(See additional lyrics)*

streets of La - re - do, as I walked
you are a cow - boy", these words he did
used to go dash - ing, with no one as
car - ry my cof - fin, and six pret - ty
play the fife low - ly, and play the dead

out in La - re - do one day, I
say as I calm - ly went by. "Come
quick on the trig - ger as I. I
maid - ens to sing a sad song, I take
march as they car - ry my pall. Put

Additional Lyrics

6. "Go gather around you a crowd of young cowboys,
And tell them the story of this my sad fate.
Tell one and the other before they go further,
To stop their wild roving before it's too late."

7. "Go fetch me a cup, just a cup of cold water,
To cool my parched lips," the cowboy then said.
Before I returned, his brave spirit had left him,
And, gone to his Maker, the cowboy was dead.

SWEET BETSY FROM PIKE

American Folksong

1. Oh, don't you re-mem-ber sweet
2.-8. *See additional lyrics*

Bet - sy from Pike, who crossed the big moun-tains with her lov-er Ike; with

two yoke of cat - tle, a large yel-low dog, a ___ tall Shang-hai roos - ter, and

one spot-ted hog, say-ing good-bye, Pike Coun-ty, fare-well for a-while. We'll

come back a-gain when we've panned out our pile. (2.-8.) panned out our pile.

Additional Lyrics

2. One evening quite early they camped on the Platte,
   'Twas near by the road on a green shady flat,
   Where Betsy, sore-footed, lay down to repose —
   With wonder Ike gazed on that Pike County rose.
   To Chorus

3. Their wagon broke down with a terrible crash,
   And out on the prairie rolled all kinds of trash,
   A few little baby clothes done up with care,
   'Twas rather suspicious, but all on the square.
   To Chorus

4. The Shanghai ran off, and their cattle all died;
   That morning the last piece of bacon was fried;
   Poor Ike was discouraged and Betsy got mad,
   The dog drooped his tail and looked wondrously sad.
   To Chorus

5. They soon reached the desert where Betsy gave out,
   And down in the sand she lay rolling about;
   While Ike, half distracted, looked on with surprise,
   Saying, "Betsy, get up, you'll get sand in your eyes."
   To Chorus

6. Sweet Betsy got up in a great deal of pain,
   Declared she'd go back to Pike County again;
   But Ike gave a sigh, and they fondly embraced,
   And they travelled along with his arm 'round her waist.
   To Chorus

7. They suddenly stopped on a very high hill,
   With wonder looked down upon old Placerville;
   Ike sighed when he said, and he cast his eyes down,
   "Sweet Betsy, my darling, we've got to Hangtown."
   To Chorus

8. Long Ike and sweet Betsy attended a dance;
   Ike wore a pair of his Pike County pants;
   Sweet Betsy was dressed up in ribbons and rings;
   Says Ike, "You're an angel, but where are your wings?"
   To Chorus

THERE IS A TAVERN IN THE TOWN

Drinking Song, originally from Cornwall, England
transcribed by WILLIAM HILLS, 1883

Dm7   G7   Am   G7   C   F

free,   And   nev -   er   nev - er   thinks   of   me. _____

me,   Takes   this   dark   dam - sel   on   his   knee. _____

C   CHORUS   G7   C

Fare   thee   well   for   I   must   leave   thee,   do   not   let   the   part - ing

f

G7   C   F

grieve   thee,   And   re - mem - ber   that   the   best   of   friends   must   part,   must

C

part.   A - dieu,   a - dieu, kind   friends   a - dieu,   A - dieu,   a - dieu,   I

3. And now I see him nevermore, nevermore.
   He never knocks upon my door, on my door.
   Oh, woe is me, he pinned a little note,
   And these were all the words he wrote:
   (CHORUS)

4. Oh, dig my grave both wide and deep, wide and deep.
   Put tombstones at my head and feet, head and feet.
   And on my breast you may carve a turtle dove,
   To signify I died for love.
   (CHORUS)

THE WABASH CANNON BALL

Hobo Song, c. 1880s

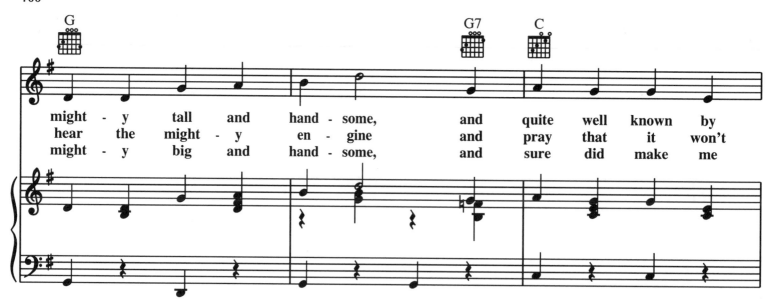

might - y tall and hand - some, and quite well known by
hear the might - y en - gine and pray that it won't
might - y big and hand - some, and sure did make me

all, How we love the choo choo of the
stall, While we safe - ly trav - el on the
fall, He's a - com - ing tow'rd me on the

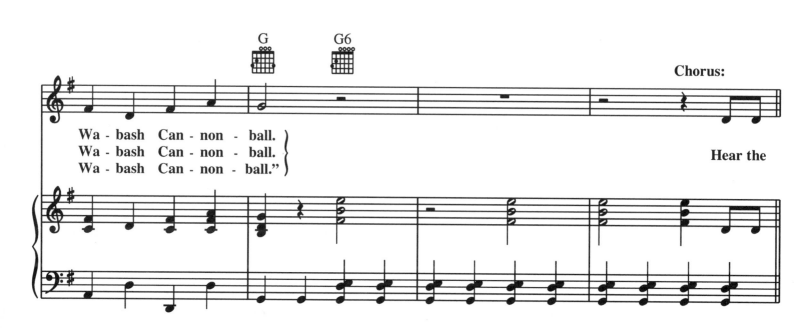

Wa - bash Can - non - ball. }
Wa - bash Can - non - ball. }
Wa - bash Can - non - ball." }

Chorus:

Hear the

TURKEY IN THE STRAW

American Folksong

Bright hoedown tempo

As___ I was a go- in' on___ down the road, with a
Went___ out to milk and I did-n't know how, I

tired team and a hea- vy load, I___ cracked my___ whip___ and the
milked the goat___ in- stead of the cow, a___ mon- key___ sit- tin' on a

lead- er sprung; I___ says day- day___ to the wag- on tongue.
pile of straw a- wink- in' at___ his moth- er- in- law.

3. Met Mr. Catfish comin' down stream,
   Says Mr. Catfish, "What does you mean?"
   Caught Mr. Catfish by the snout
   And turned Mr. Catfish wrong side out.
   Chorus:

4. Came to the river and I couldn't get across,
   Paid five dollars for an old blind hoss
   Wouldn't go ahead, nor he wouldn't stand still,
   So he went up and down like an old saw mill.
   Chorus:

5. As I came down the new cut road
   Met Mr. Bullfrog, met Miss Toad,
   And every time Miss Toad would sing
   Ole Bullfrog cut a pigeon wing.
   Chorus:

6. Oh, I jumped in the seat, and I gave a little yell,
   The horses run away, broke the wagon all to hell;
   Sugar in the gourd and honey in the horn,
   I never was so happy since the hour I was born.
   Chorus:

CHORUS
Turkey in the straw, turkey in the hay,
Roll 'em up and twist 'em up a high tuckahaw,
And hit 'em up a tune called Turkey in the Straw.

WHEN JOHNNY COMES MARCHING HOME

Words and Music by LOUIS LAMBERT,
pen name for PATRICK GILMORE
written in 1863, melody adapted
from an Irish folksong
(Gilmore was bandmaster of the Union army.)

Moving along, in 2

When John - ny comes march - ing home a - gain, Hur - rah! _____ Hur - rah! _____ we'll give him a heart - y wel - come then, Hur -

WHEN THE SAINTS GO MARCHING IN

New Orleans Gospel Song,
possibly originally from the Bahamas;
in 1896 two writers claimed authorship of the song:
KATHERINE E. PURVIS (words) and
JAMES M. BLACK (music)

WONDROUS LOVE

Southern American Folk Hymn,
17th or 18th century

Moderately

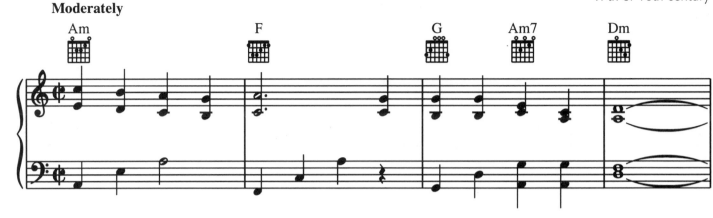

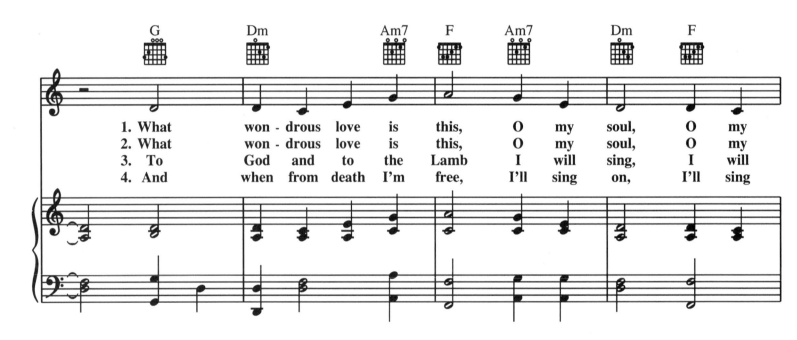

1. What won-drous love is this, O my soul, O my
2. What won-drous love is this, O my soul, O my
3. To God and to the Lamb I will sing, O I will
4. And when from death I'm free, I'll sing on, I'll sing

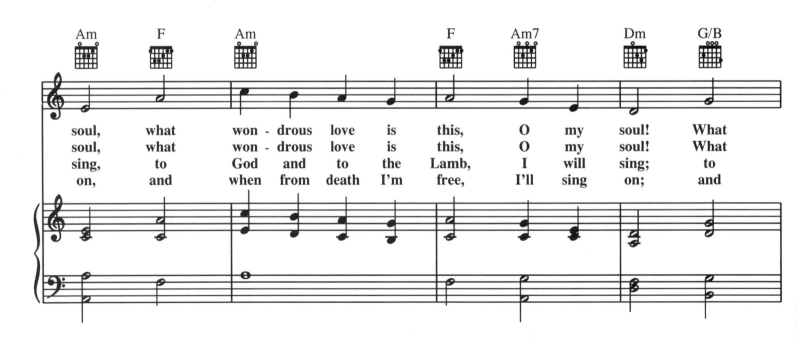

soul, what won-drous love is this, O my soul! What
soul, what won-drous love is this, O my soul! What
sing, to God and to the Lamb, I will sing; to
on, and when from death I'm free, I'll sing on; and

YANKEE DOODLE BOY

18th Century Song,
possibly originating with British soliders of
the French and Indian War; adopted and
adapted by American soldiers during
the Revolutionary War

Tempo di Marcia.

I'm the kid that's all the can - dy,
Fa - ther's name was Hez - i - ki - ah,

I'm a Yan - kee Doo - dle Dan - dy, I'm glad I am, ___
Moth - er's name was Ann Ma - ri - a, Yanks through and through.

CHORUS.

I'm a Yan - kee Doo - dle Dan - - dy, A
Yan - kee Doo - dle, do or die; A
real live nep - hew of my Un - cle Sam's,
Born on the Fourth of Ju - ly. I've

HE'S GOT THE WHOLE WORLD
IN HIS HANDS

African-American Folksong
possibly from North Carolina

ALL MY TRIALS

African-American Spiritual
from the South

DEEP RIVER

African-American Spiritual
Based on Joshua 3

DIDN'T MY LORD DELIVER DANIEL?

African-American Spiritual
from the South

NOBODY KNOWS THE TROUBLE I'VE SEEN

African-American Spiritual, c. 1850s,
from the islands off
Georgia and South Carolina

EVERY TIME I FEEL THE SPIRIT

African-American Spiritual
from the South

JACOB'S LADDER

African-American Spiritual
from the South, 17th or 18th century

JOSHUA FIT THE BATTLE OF JERICHO

African-American Spiritual
from the South

LET US BREAK BREAD TOGETHER

African-American Spiritual
from the South

Moderately slow

THIS LITTLE LIGHT OF MINE

African-American Spiritual
from the slavery period

THE LONESOME ROAD

African-American Spiritual
c. 1870s-1890s

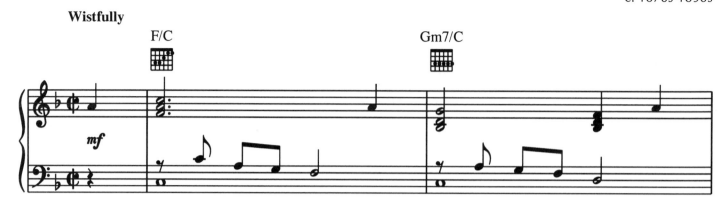

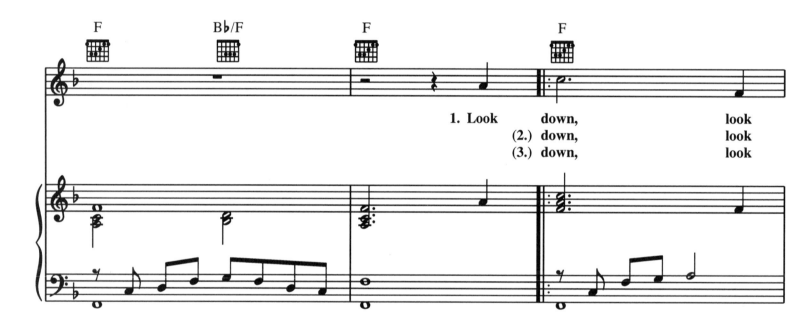

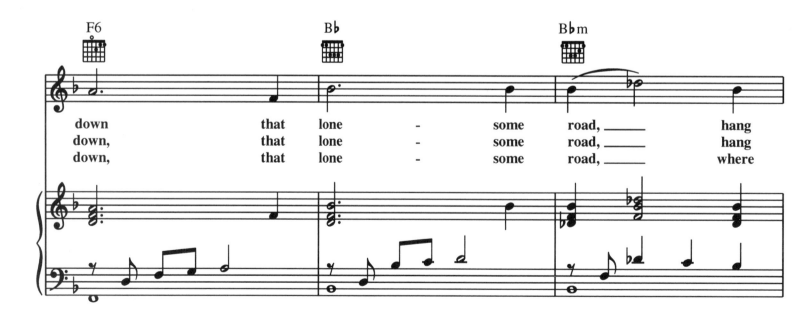

NEVER SAID A MUMBLIN' WORD

African-American Spiritual
from the South

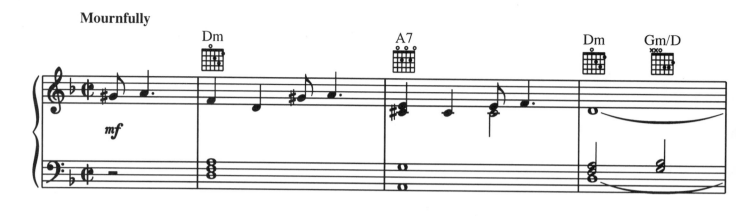

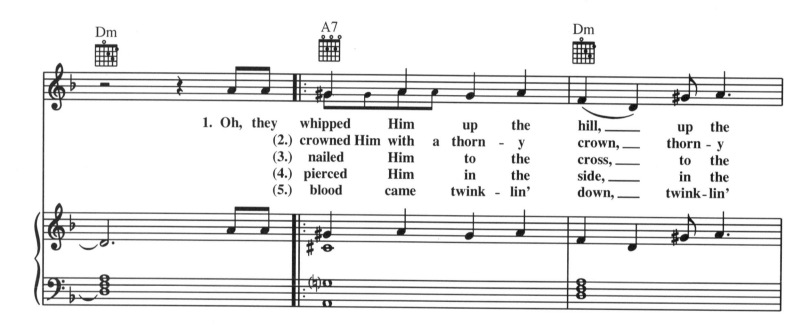

1. Oh, they whipped Him up the hill, ___ up the
(2.) crowned Him with a thorn-y crown, ___ thorn-y
(3.) nailed Him to the cross, ___ to the
(4.) pierced Him in the side, ___ in the
(5.) blood came twink-lin' down, ___ twink-lin'

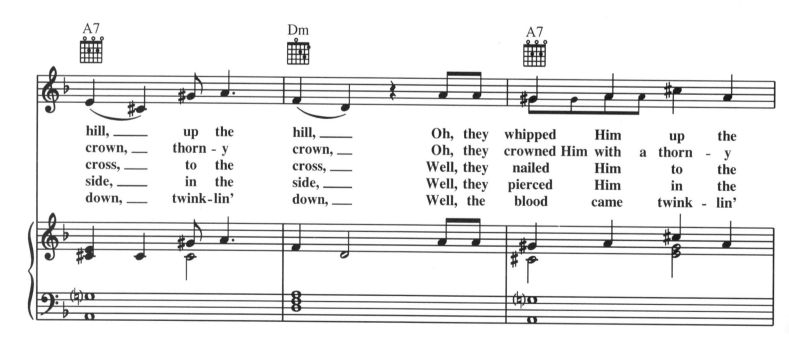

hill, ___ up the hill, ___ Oh, they whipped Him up the
crown, ___ thorn-y crown, ___ Oh, they crowned Him with a thorn-y
cross, ___ to the cross, ___ Well, they nailed Him to the
side, ___ in the side, ___ Well, they pierced Him in the
down, ___ twink-lin' down, ___ Well, the blood came twink-lin'

OH, FREEDOM

African-American Spiritual
post-Civil War

With feeling

155

ROCK-A-MY SOUL

African-American Spiritual
from the slavery period

SOMEBODY'S KNOCKIN' AT YOUR DOOR

African-American Spiritual
from the slavery period

SOMETIMES I FEEL LIKE A MOTHERLESS CHILD

African-American Spiritual
from the slavery period

SOON AH WILL BE DONE

African-American Spiritual

STANDING IN THE NEED OF PRAYER

African-American Spiritual

STEAL AWAY

African-American Spiritual
from the slavery period

Steal a - way, steal a - way, steal a - way to Je - sus. Steal a - way, steal a - way home. I ain't got long to

SWING LOW, SWEET CHARIOT

African-American Spiritual
from the slavery period

THERE IS A BALM IN GILEAD

African-American Spiritual
from the slavery period

WAYFARING STRANGER

Southern American Folk Hymn